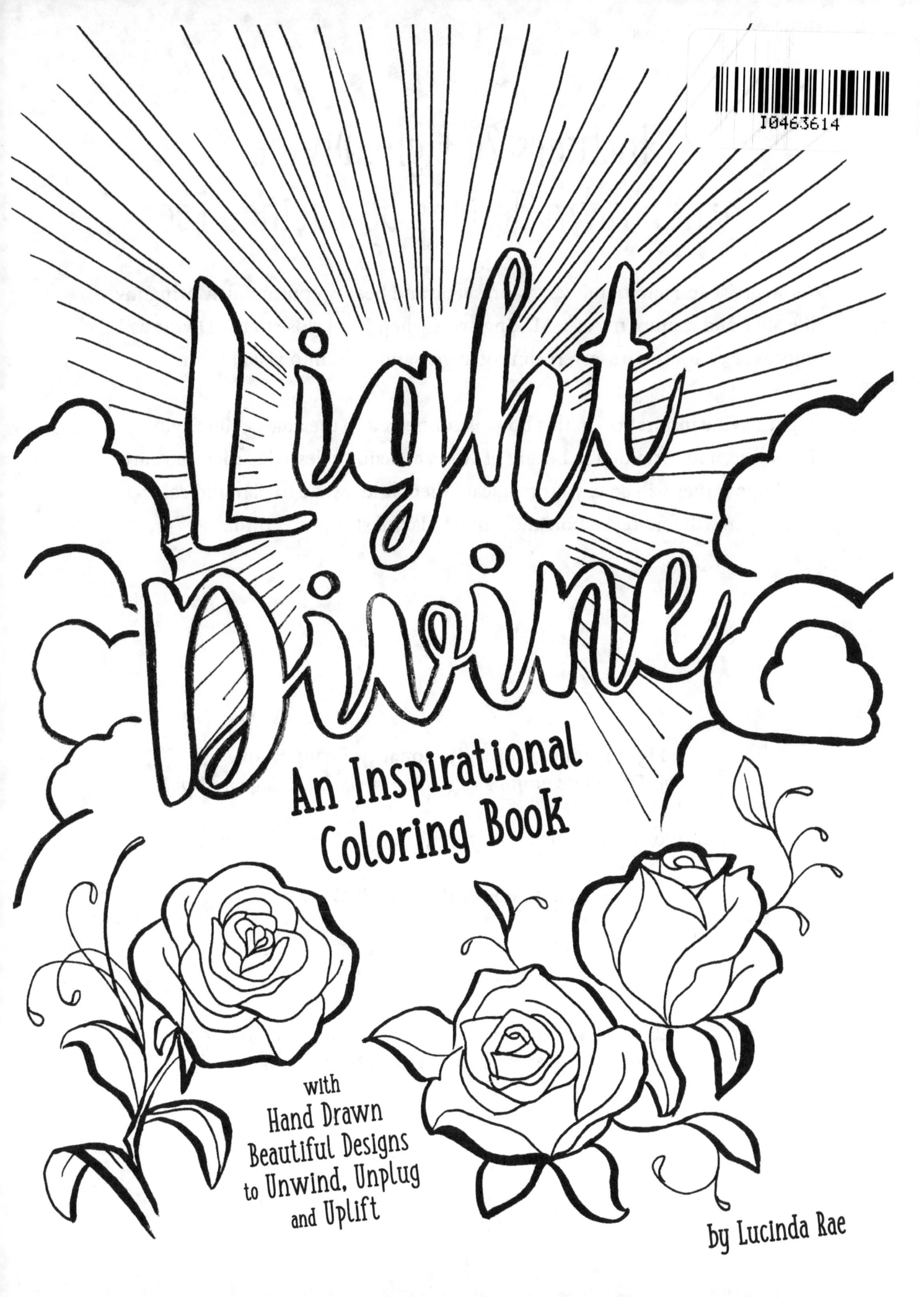

Light Divine

An Inspirational Coloring Book

with
Hand Drawn
Beautiful Designs
to Unwind, Unplug
and Uplift

by Lucinda Rae

Includes 20 Light Divine hand drawn designs by Lucinda Rae

As an artist and photographer, color, shape and beauty continuously bring my life alive and capture my eye. Making art is when I feel close to the Divine as I endeavor to awaken unseen realms of angels and light into visual form.

Light Divine inspiration in this book is connected to the angels, the Divine Feminine, and sprinkled in beauty of God's amazing celestial gardens on earth. My hope is they will coax your magical inner child awake to play and color where you will find relaxation and a quiet playful stillness within.

Light Divine: An Inspirational Coloring Book
with Hand Drawn Beautiful Designs to Unwind, Unplug and Uplift

All illustrations and publication graphic design created by Lucinda Rae.

First Published March 2017

ISBN-13: 978-1544019390
ISBN-10: 1544019394

Tips For Using This Book

I have printed the pictures on only one side for the protection of each image. You can back an image with another piece of paper you're working with in case the markers bleed through. You can use the blank space below to test out your markers or pencils.

Unplug and step away from distractions so you can relax into the peaceful, mesmerizing process and enjoy the magic of these images.

Start wherever your heart calls you! There's not need to be linear, Creative Spirit.

Play! There's no wrong or right way to bring these pages to life with color.

Pray! I heartily recommend infusing your practice of faith into these works.

This book works best with colored pencils or markers. Wet mediums to be used sparingly.

Don't be timid to move pages around and take pages out. You can cut finished pages out to frame so you and a friend can color together.

Share your work! Share on Instagram or Facebook with #ColorLucinda to be included in my gallery and visit the gallery for inspiration here: www.Lucinda-Rae/colorlucindagallery

Share your art with me...
I'll share with the world.

f
/Lucinda.Rae

Stay in touch...
www.Lucinda-Rae.com

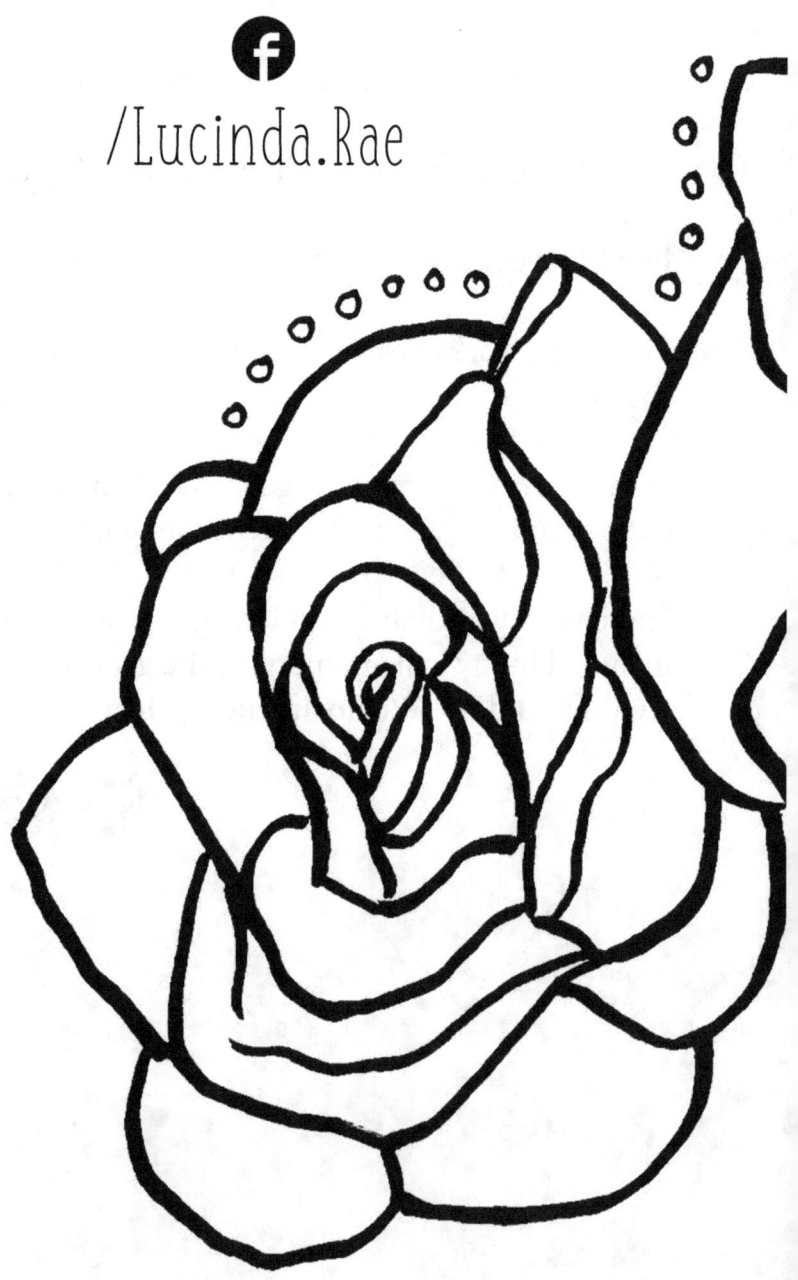

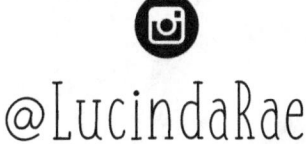

@LucindaRae

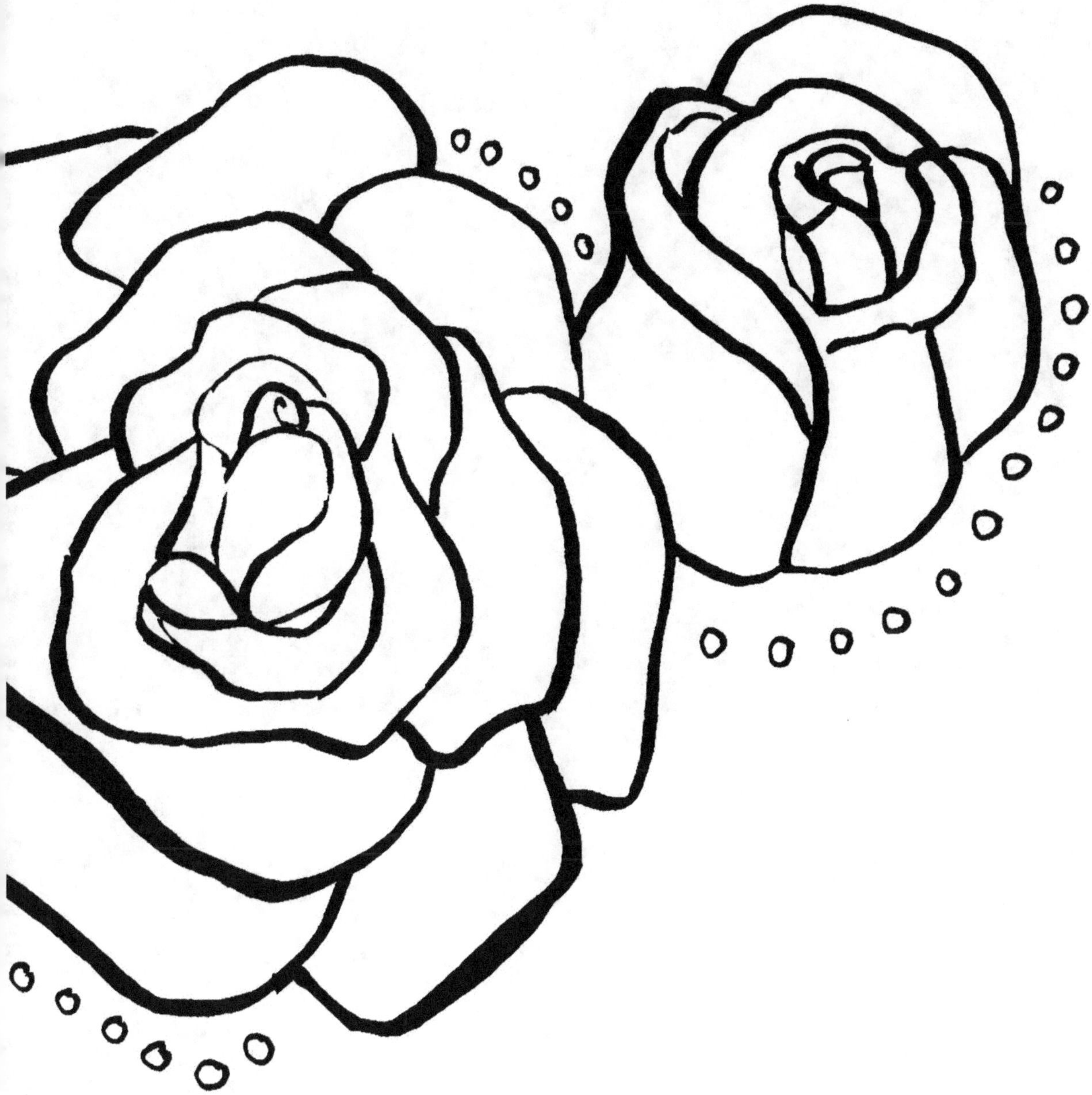

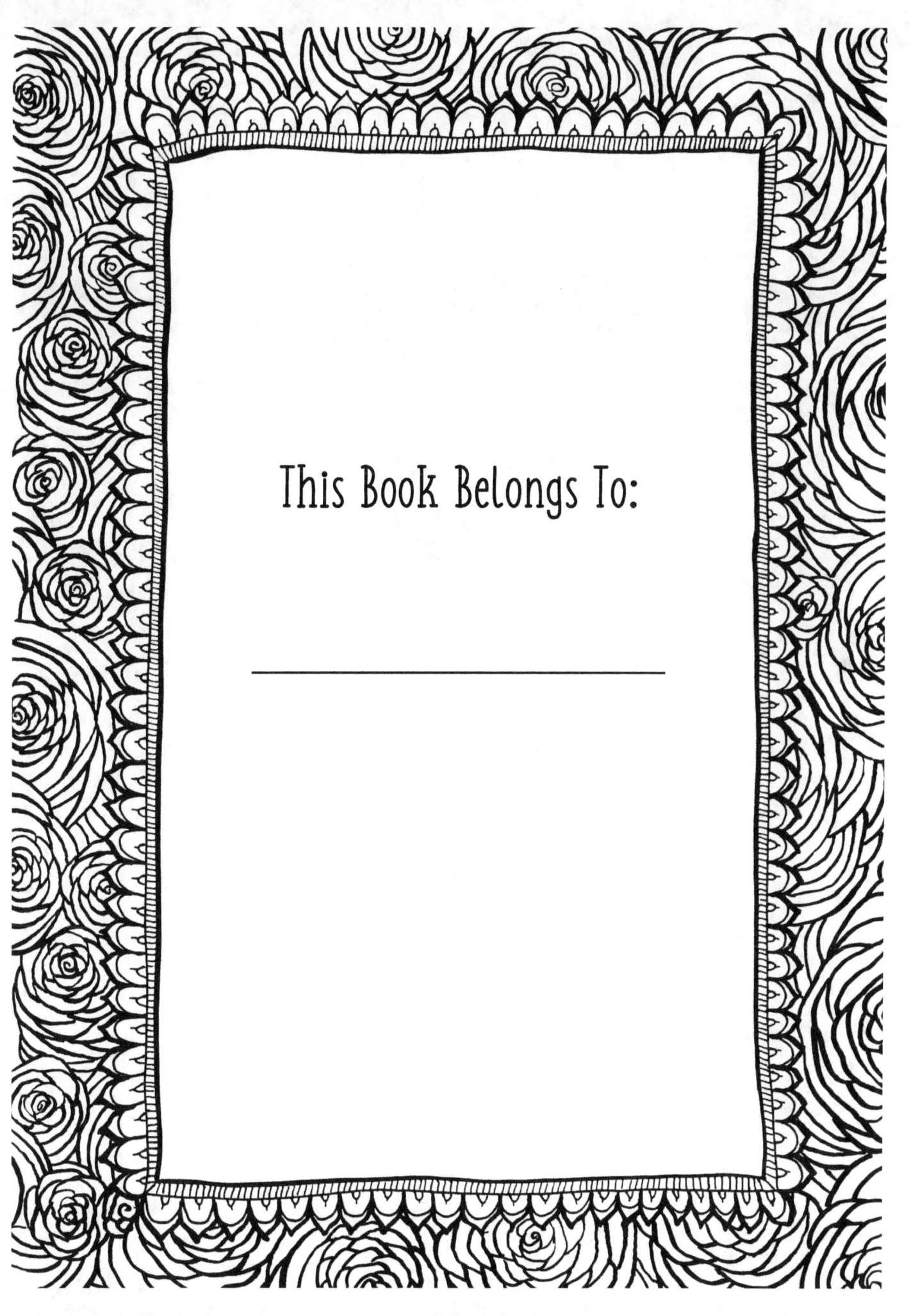

This Book Belongs To:

_____

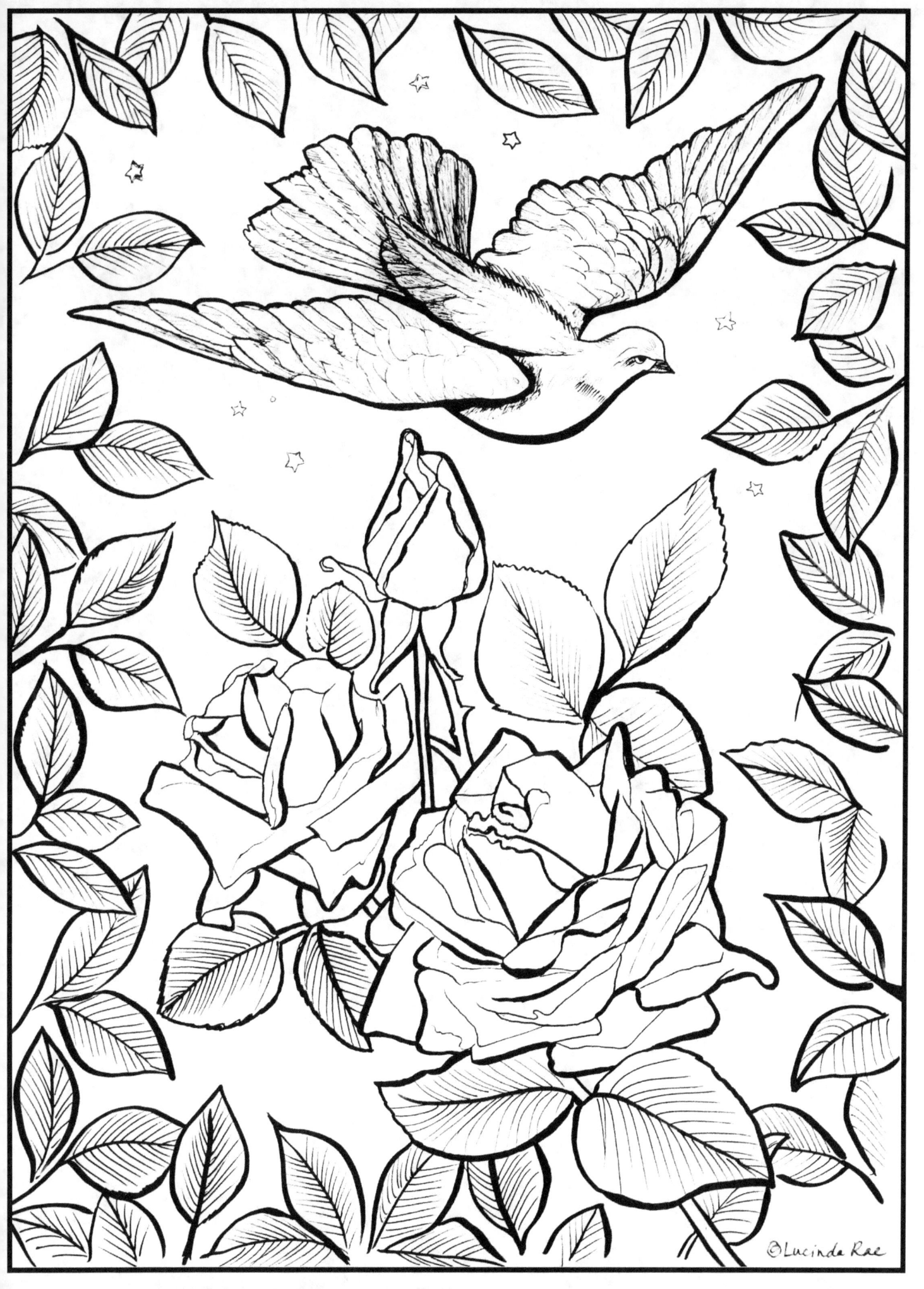
©Lucinda Rae

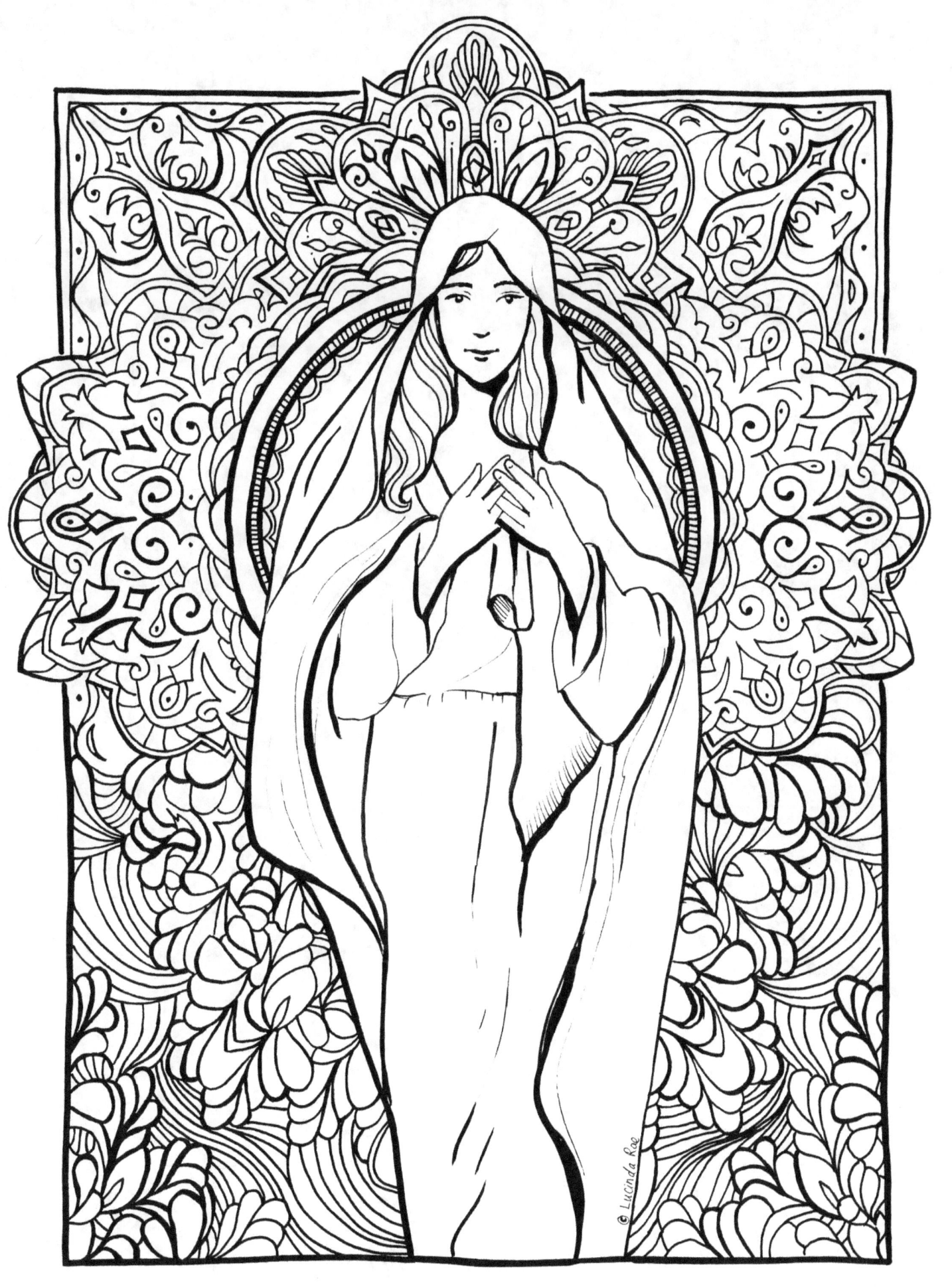

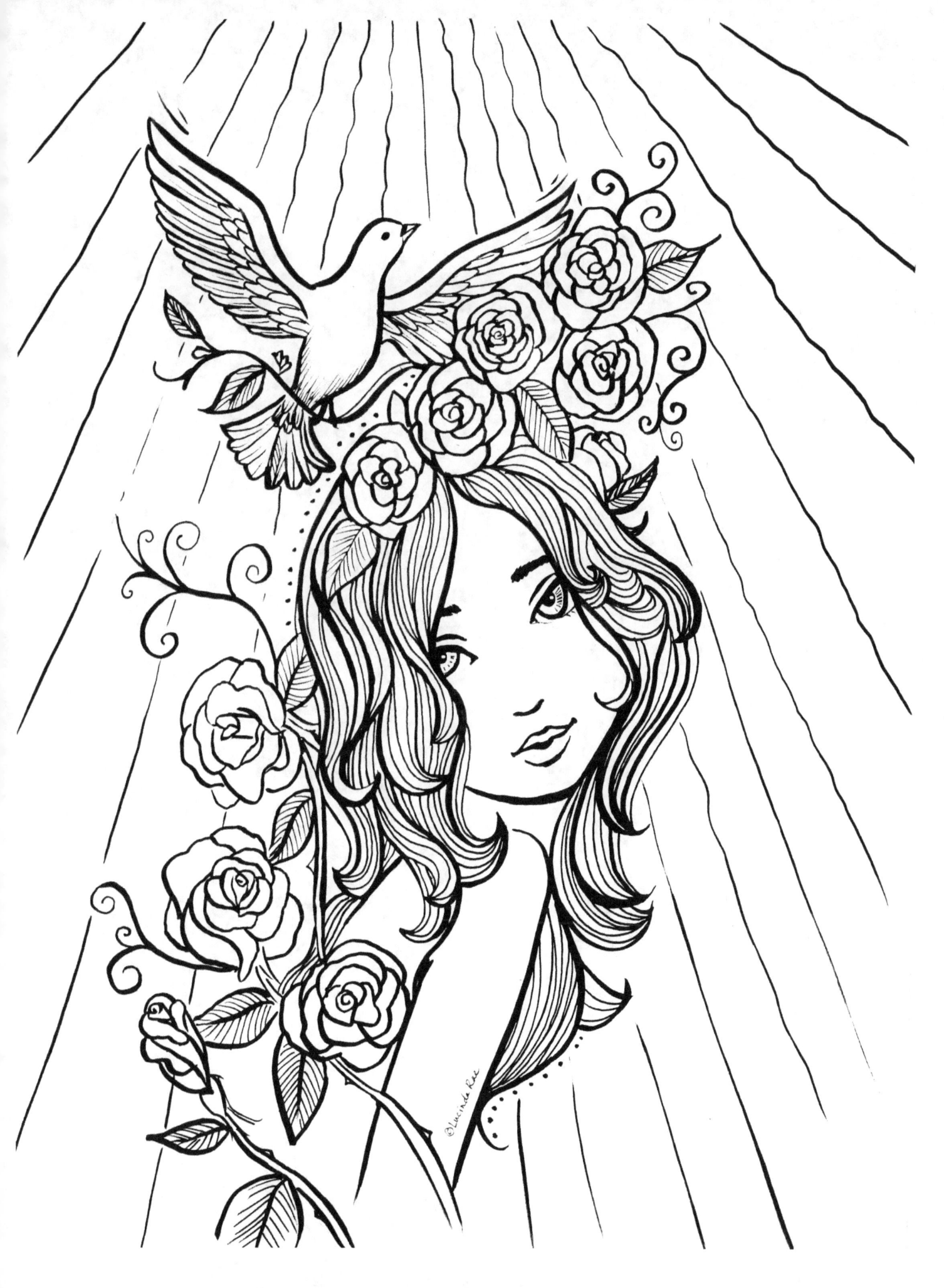

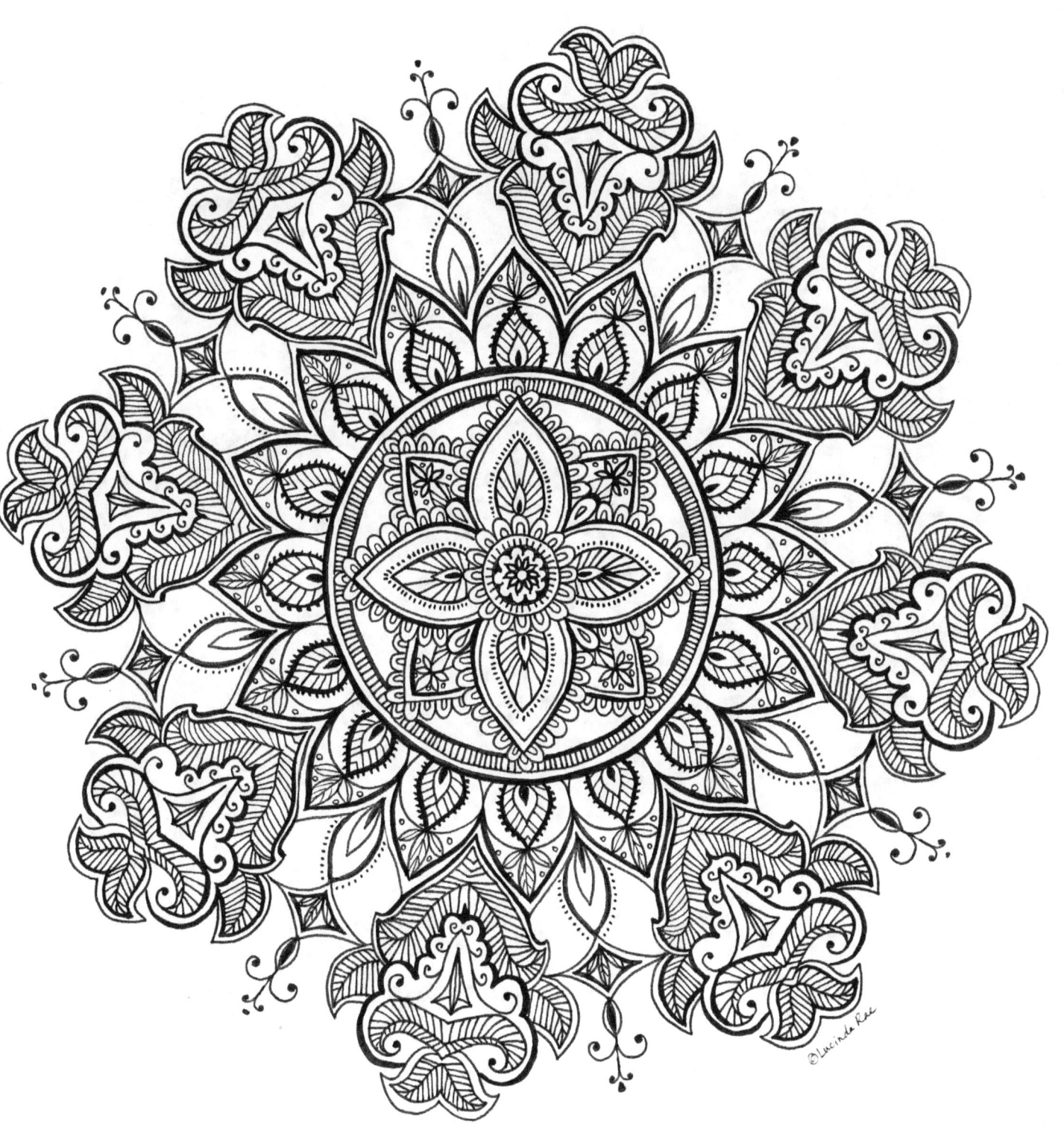

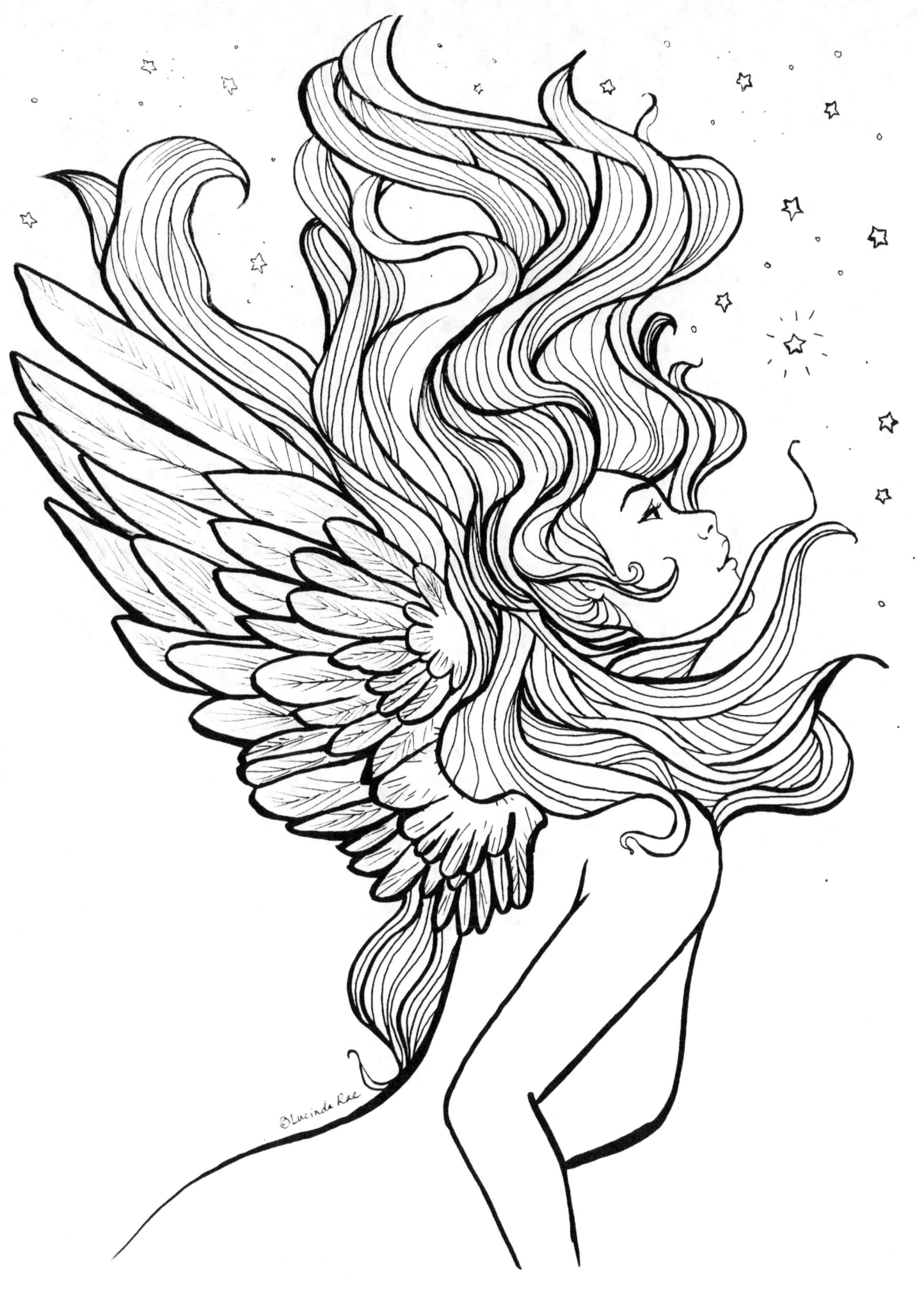

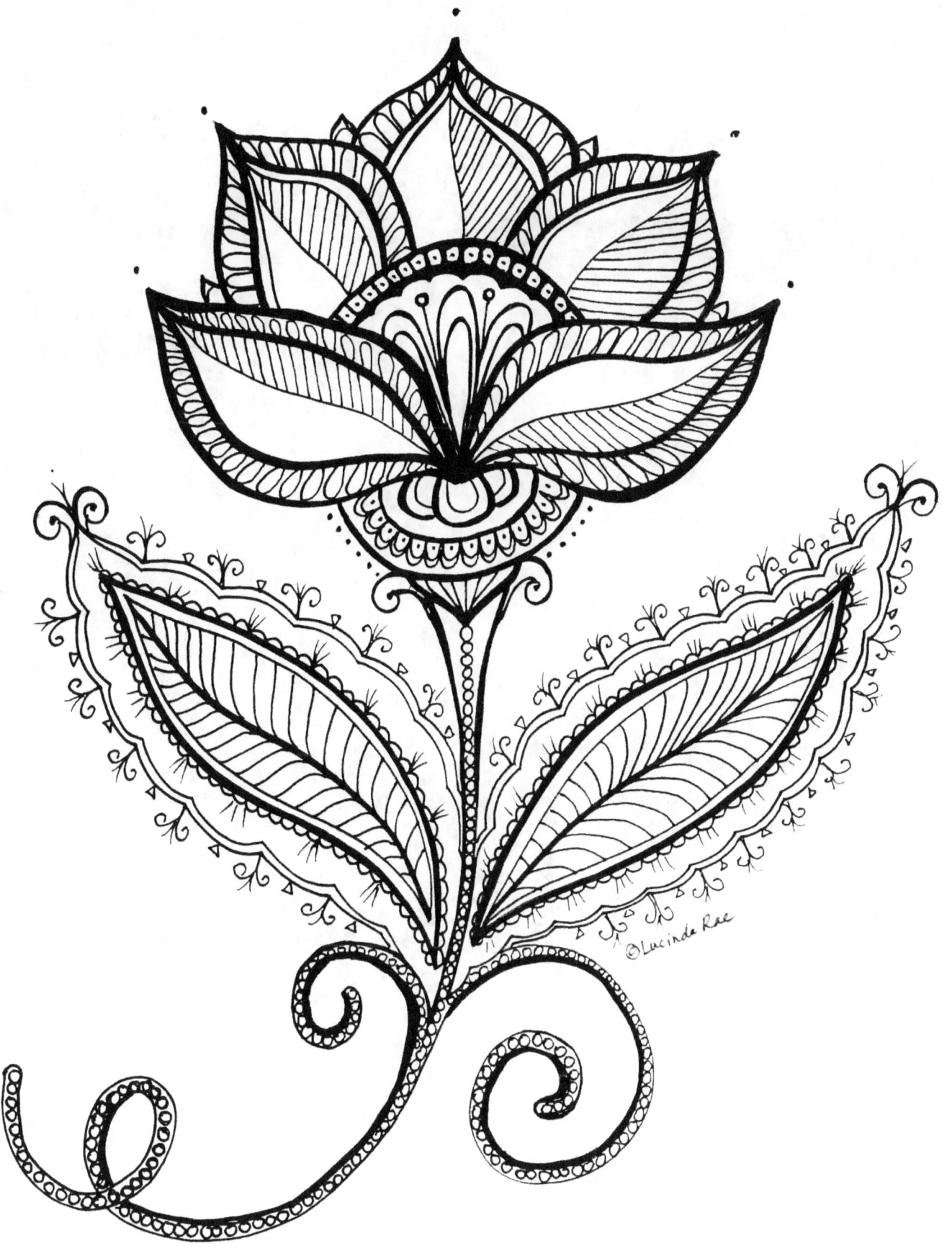

©Lucinda Rae

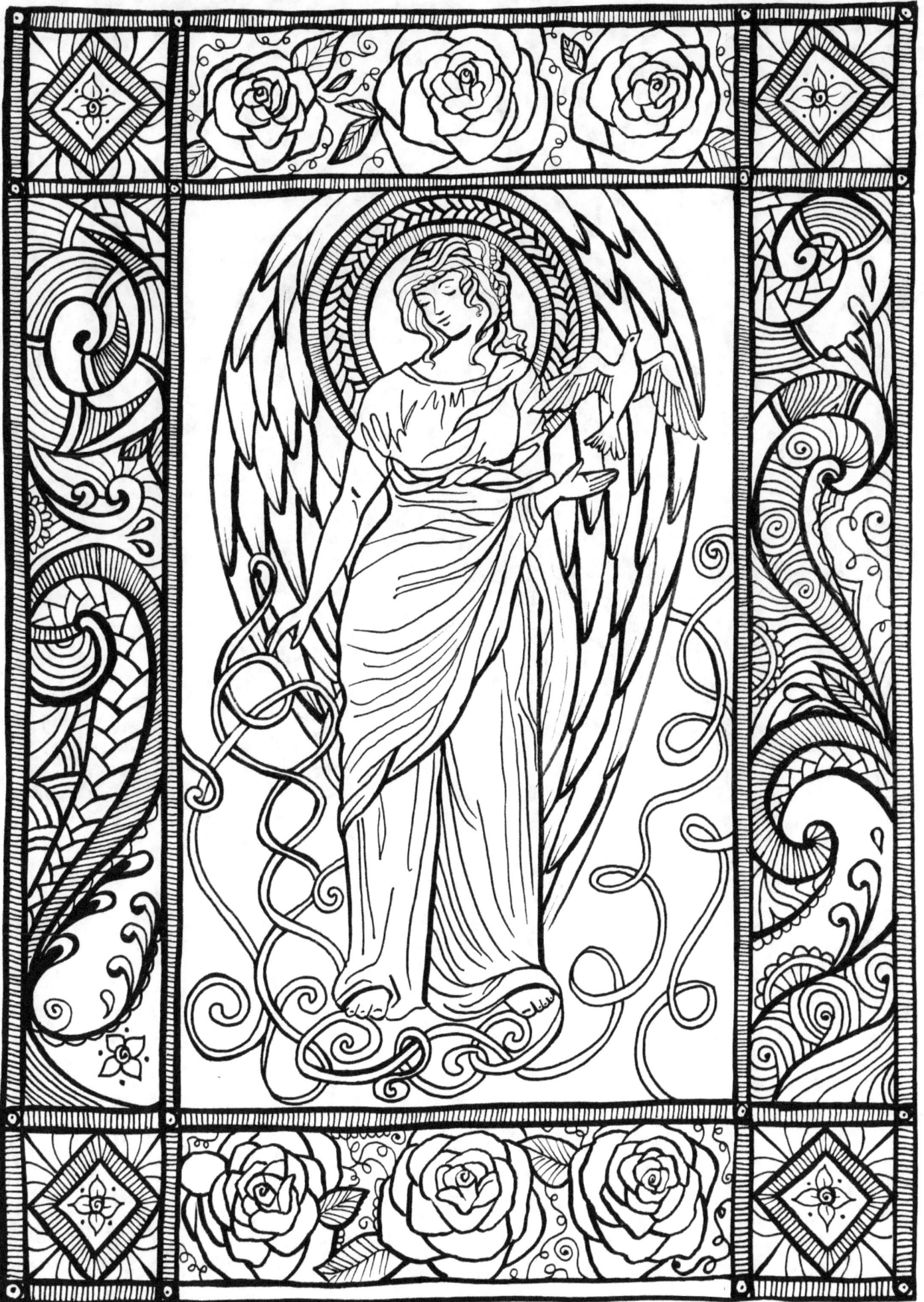

©Lucinda Rae

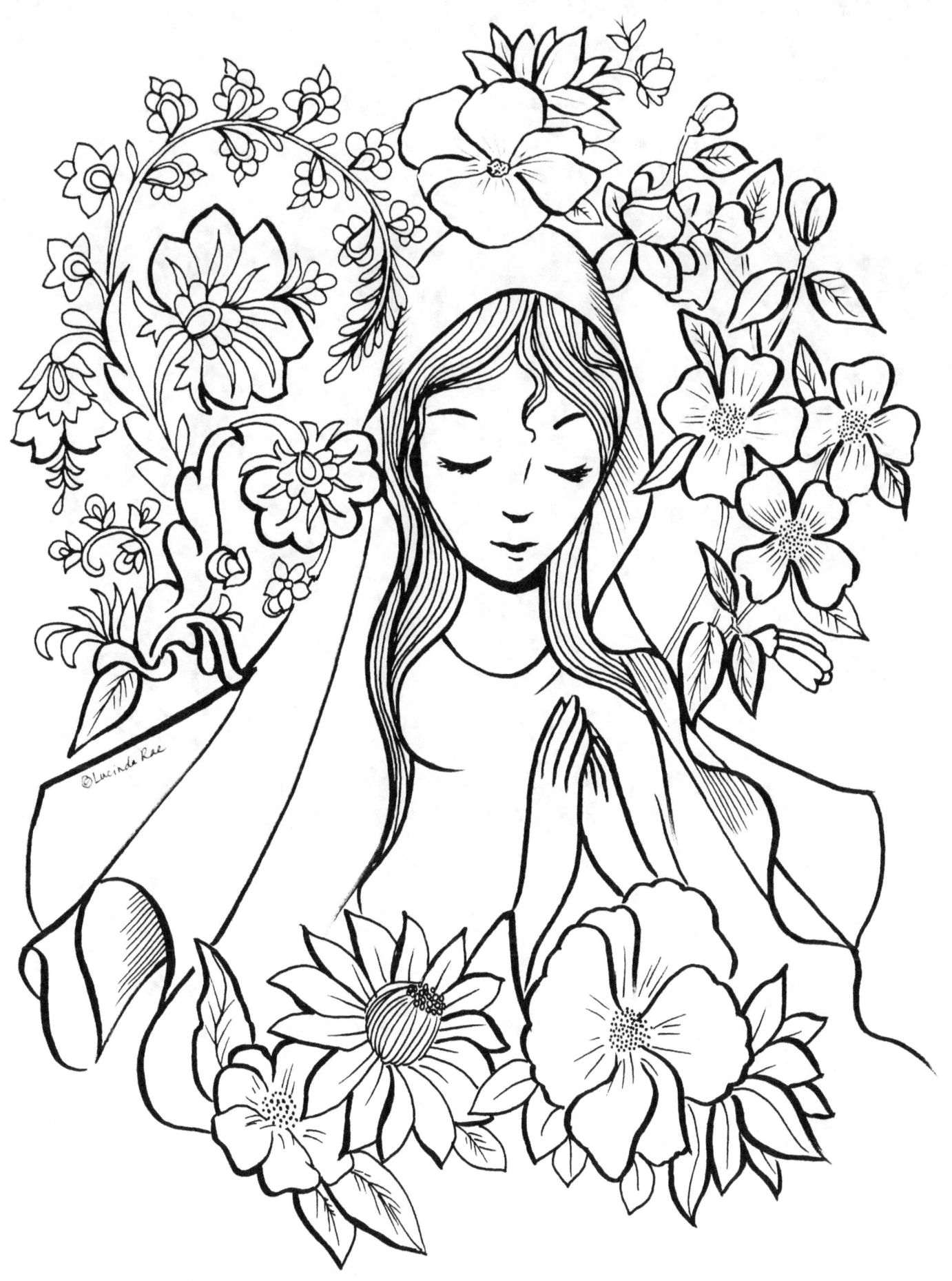

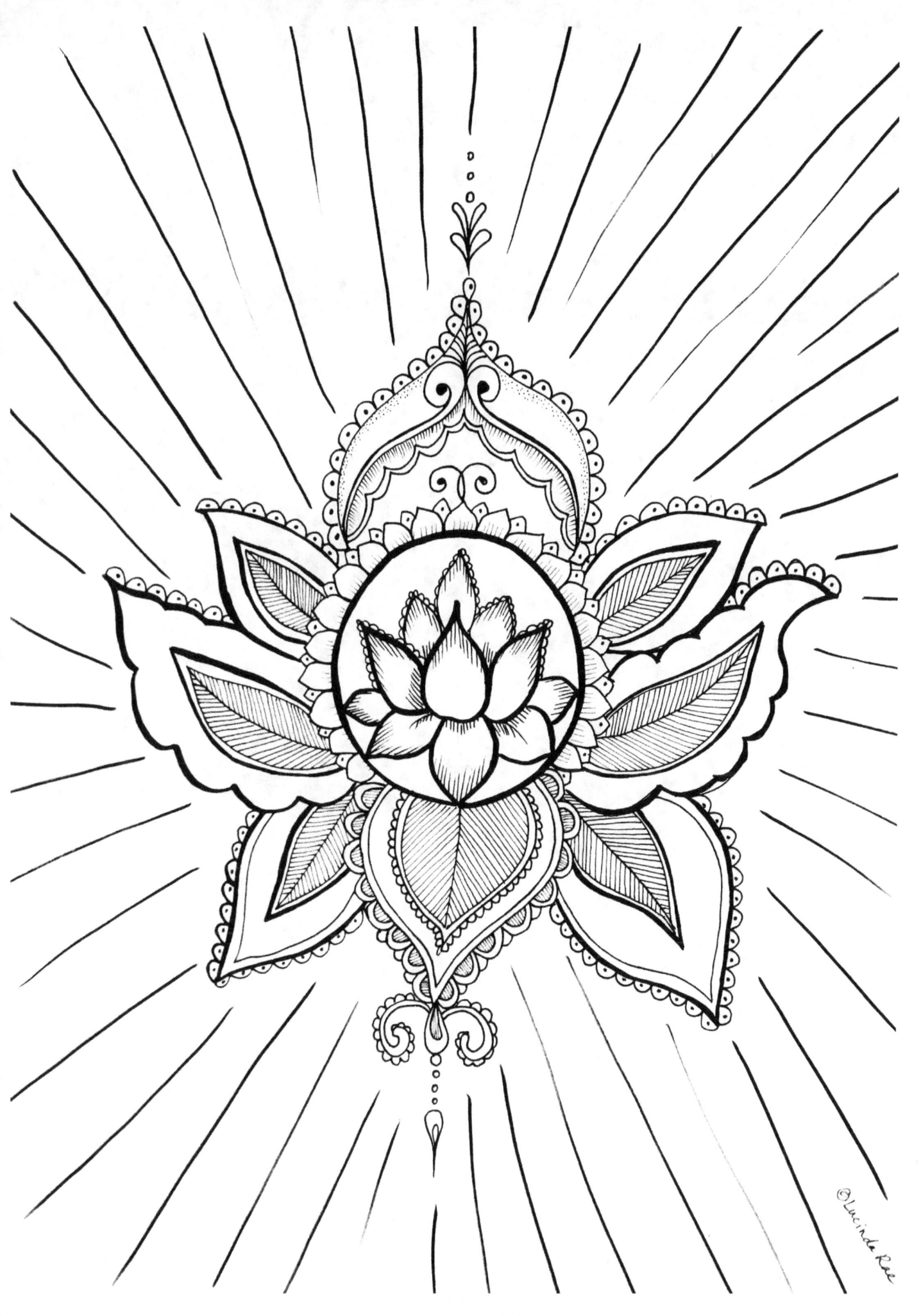

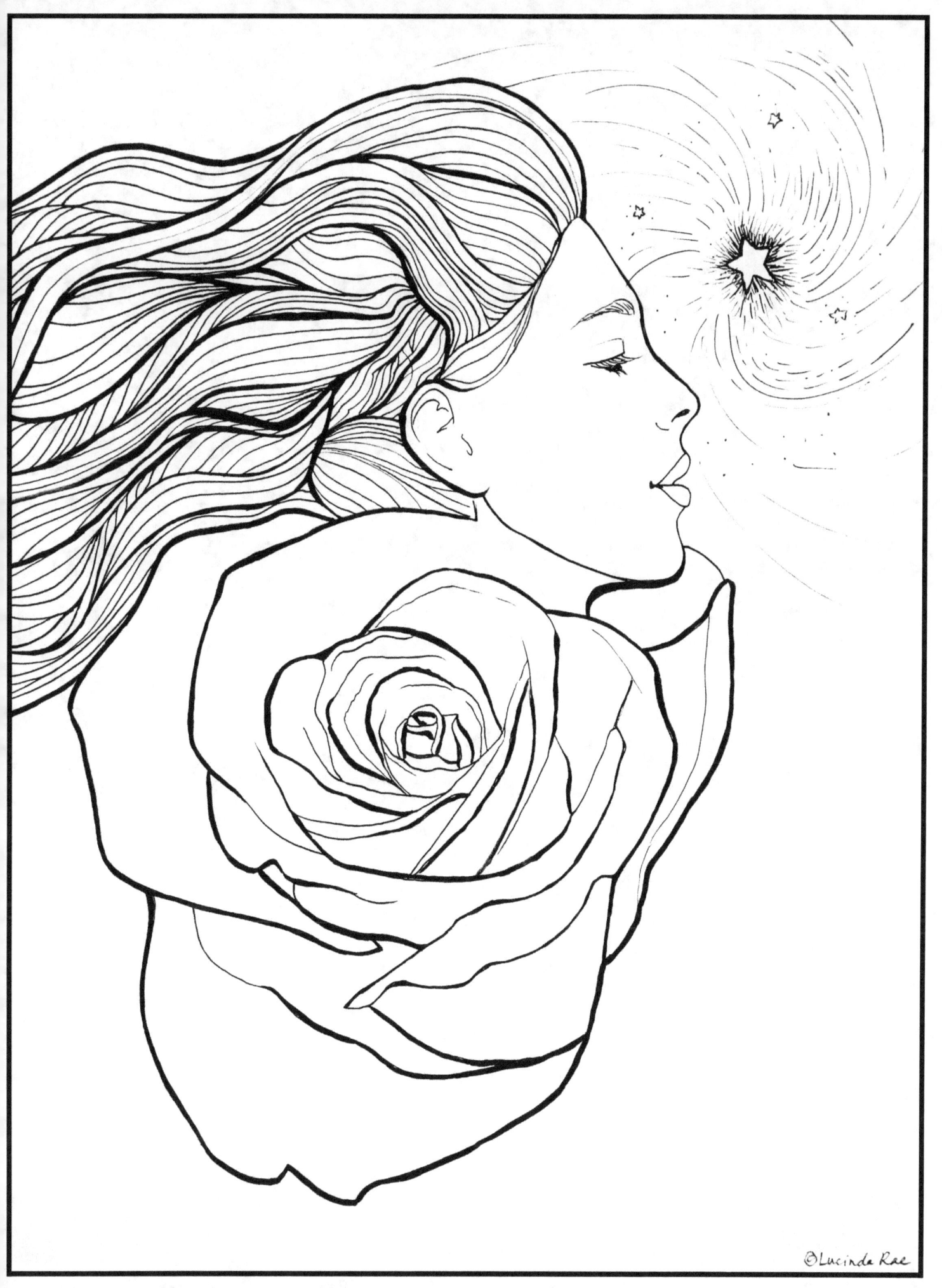

©Lucinda Rae

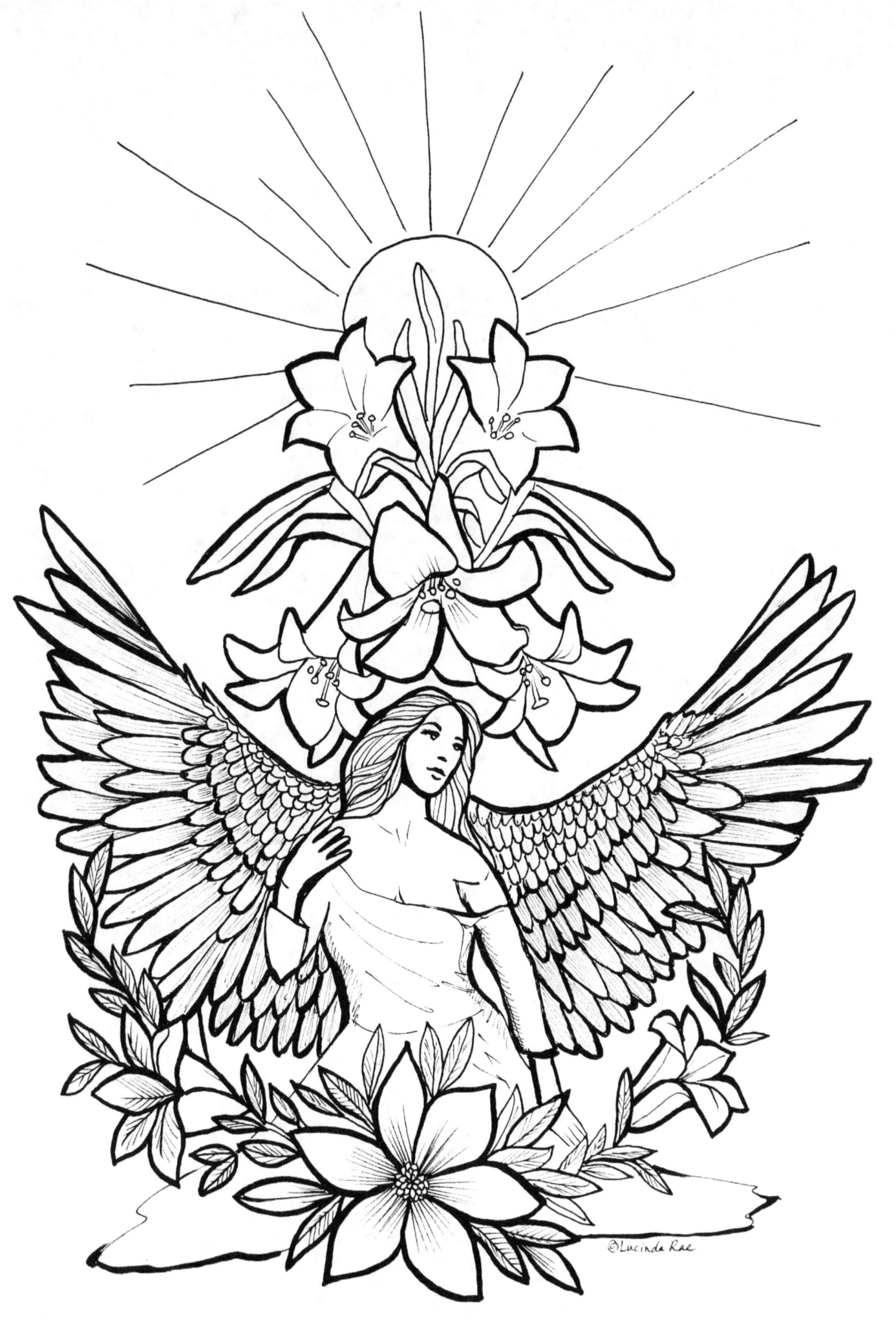

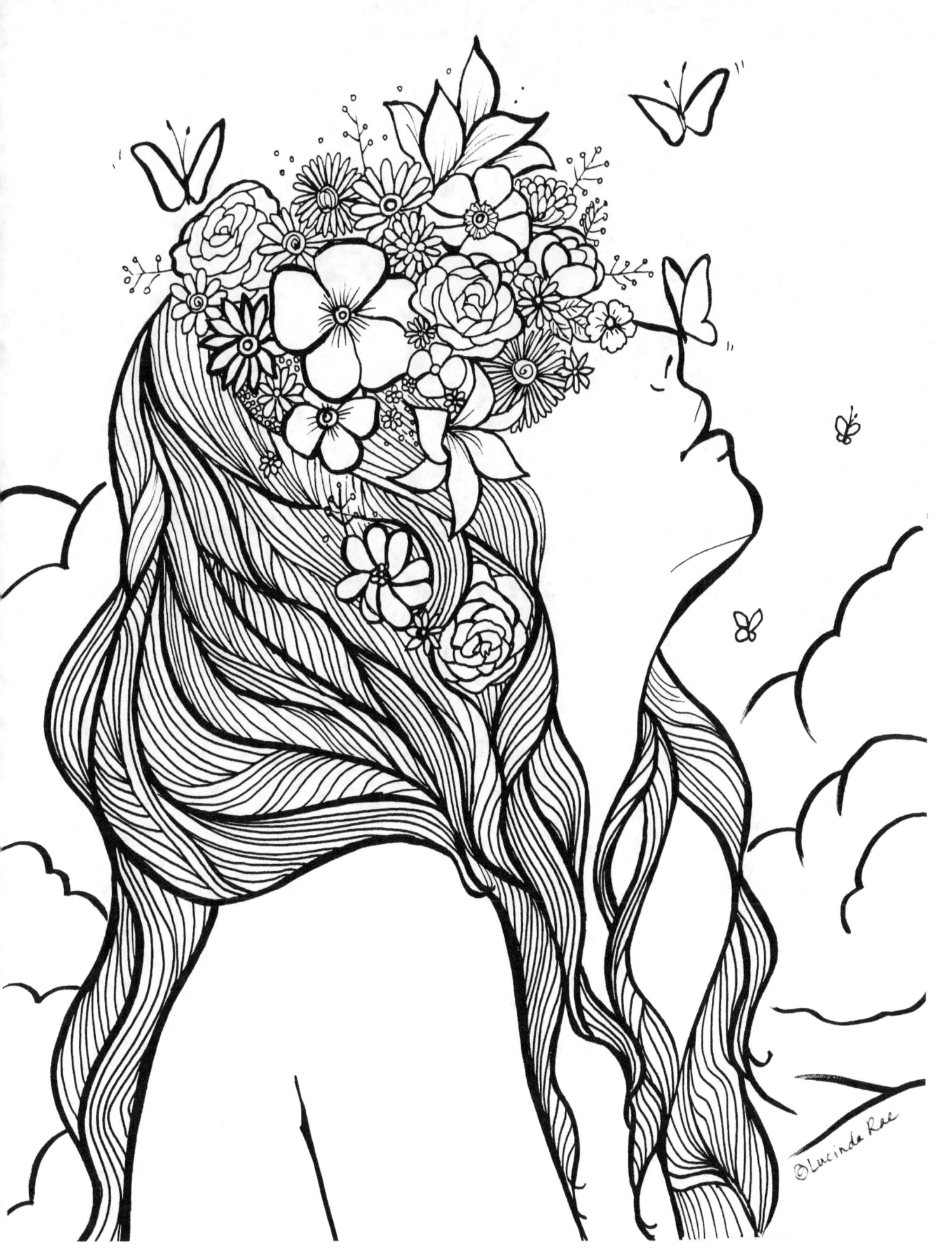

©Lucinda Ree

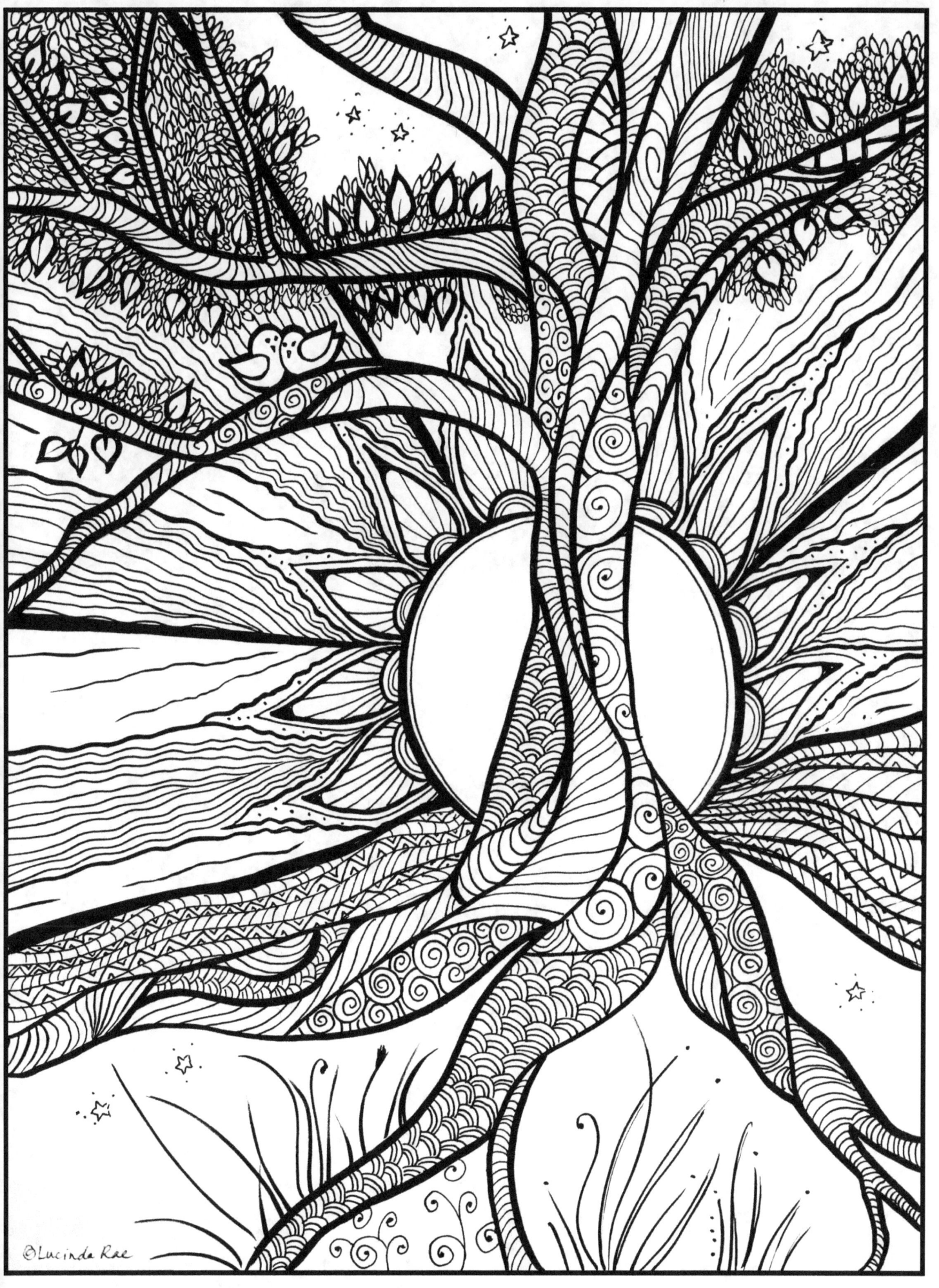

©Lucinda Rae

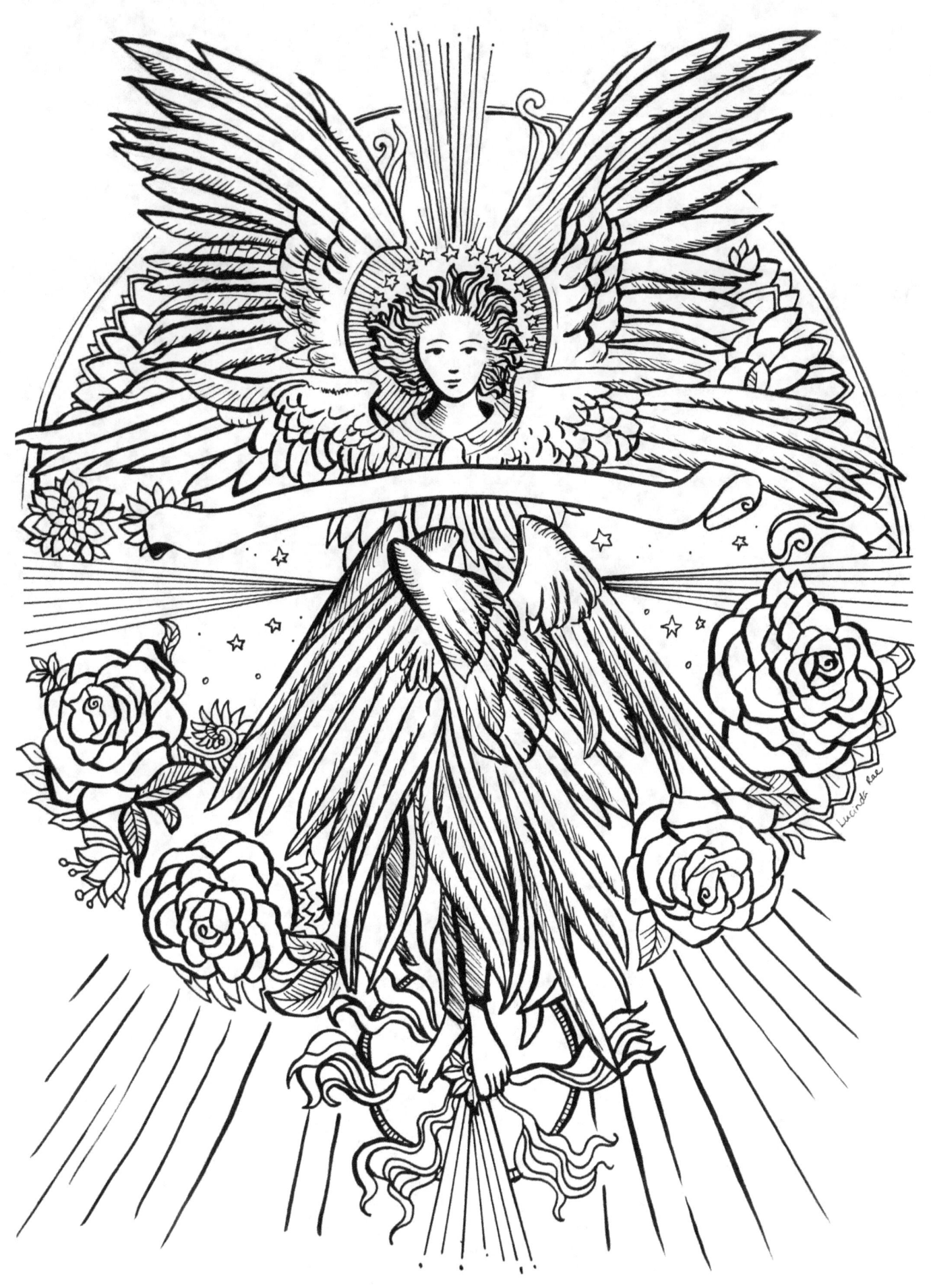

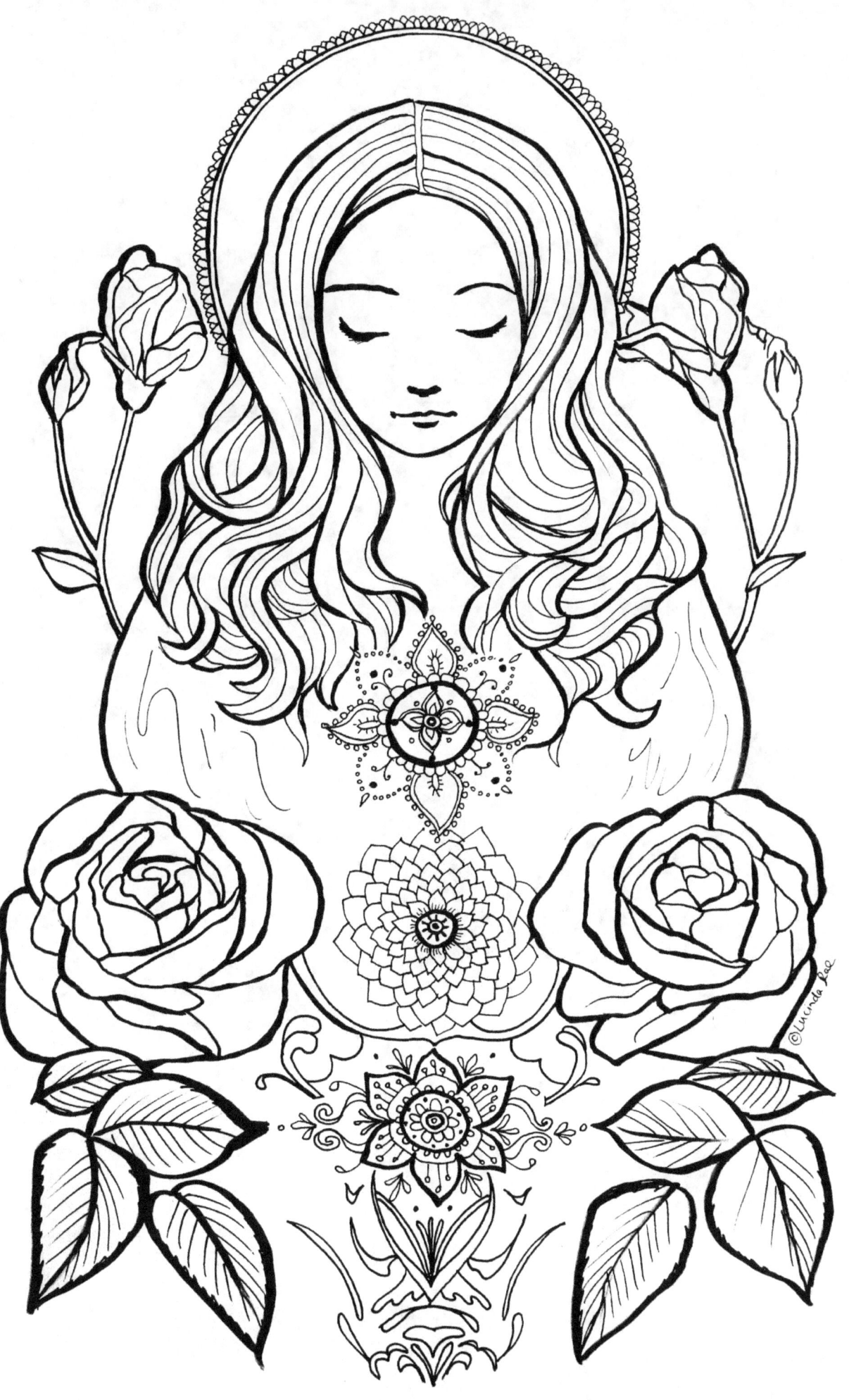

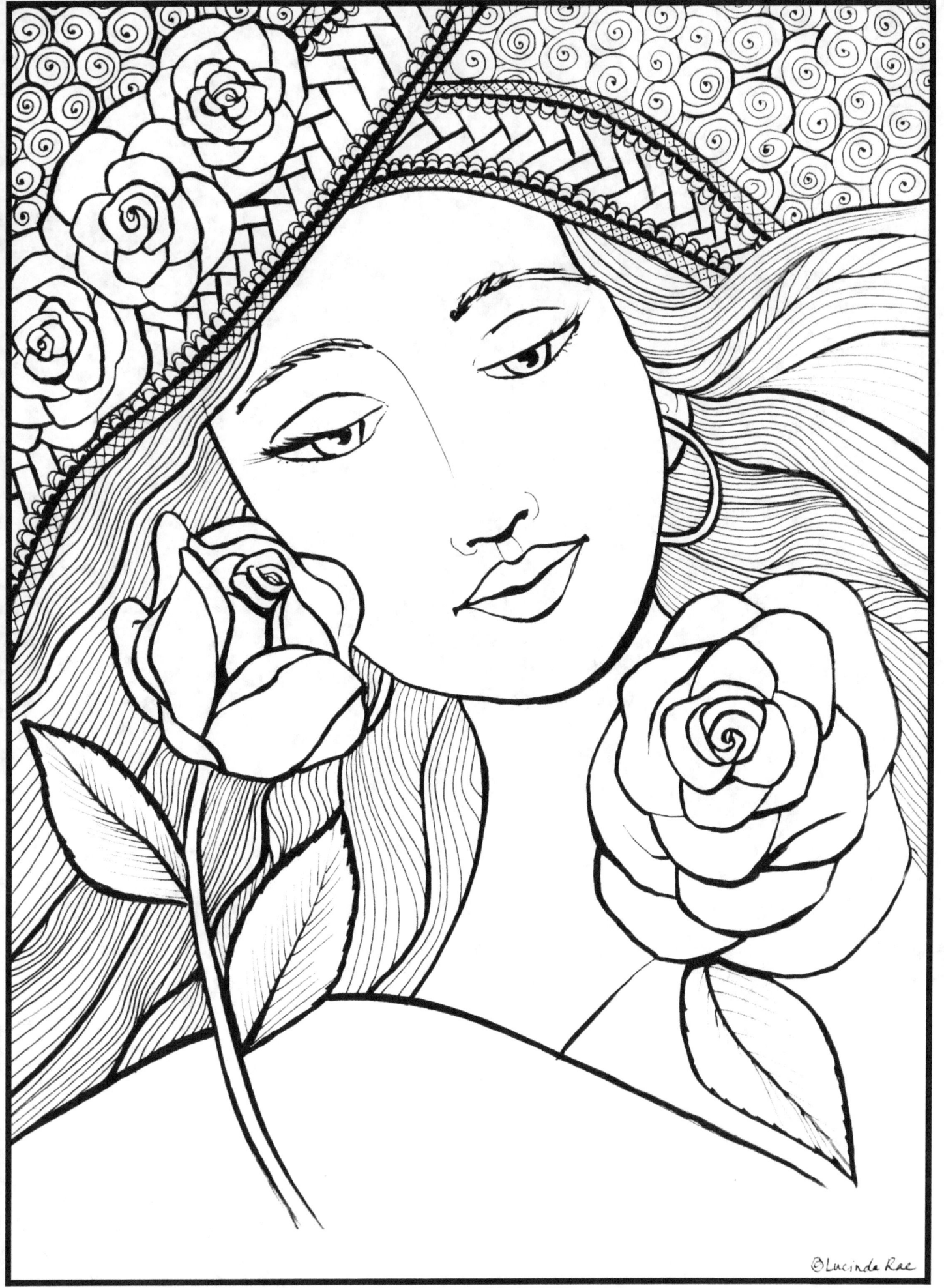

©Lucinda Rae

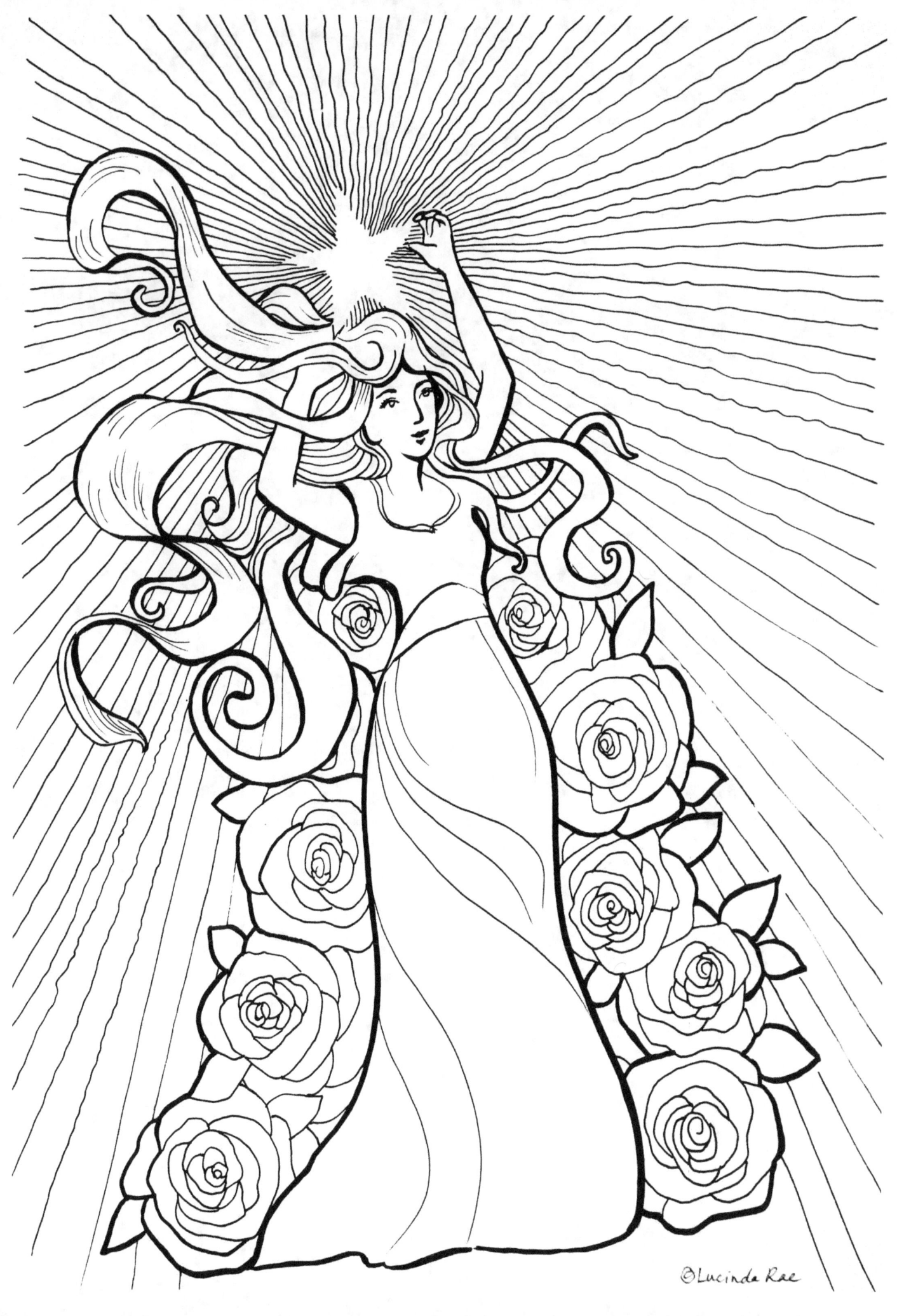

©Lucinda Rae

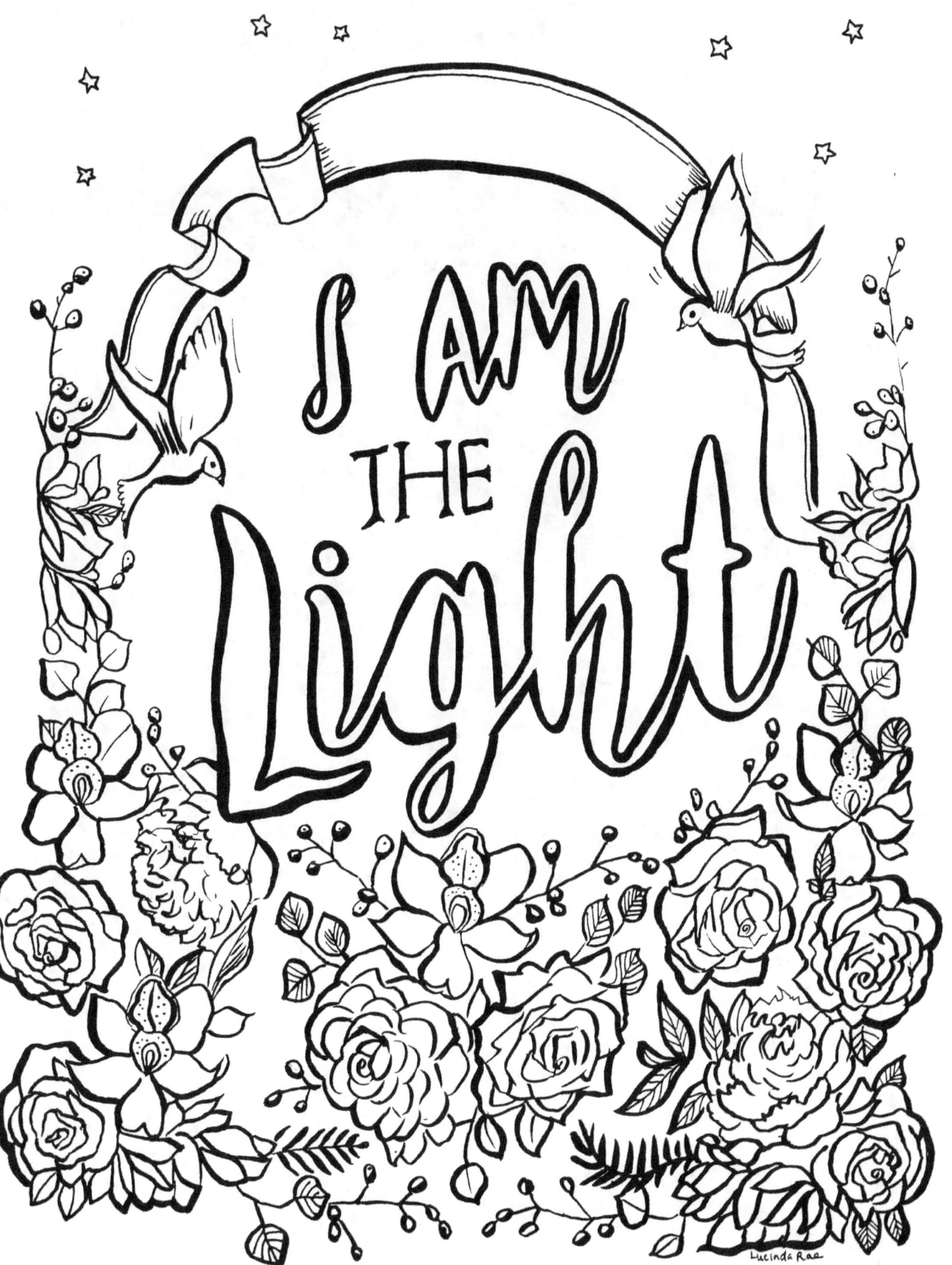

www.ingramcontent.com/pod-product-compliance
Lightning Source LLC
Chambersburg PA
CBHW081801170526
45167CB00008B/3285